Acknowledgments

I want to thank the following people for their support, encouragement, and expertise. Their suggestions were invaluable.

Doug Prestine, my husband, best friend, and computer expert

Ginger Murphy, publisher and ego booster

Kristin Eclov, editor and advisor

Lisa Schwimmer, copyeditor and good listener

Virginia Kylberg, gifted artist

Marek/Janci Design and Lucyna Green, whose cover and book designs brought the words to life

Patsy Loyd, Sales Manager for Fearon Teacher Aids

Sandy Hatch and Ann Alper, marriage, family, and child counselors

Debbie Kachidurian, Davida Kristy, Joann Burch, Pilar Holtrop, and Betsy Jackson, teachers

Cathy Lawless, elementary school principal

Nadine Davidson, Celeste Mannis, and Karen Eustis, fellow authors

The Prestine and Singleton families for their encouragement

HELPING CHILDREN SHARE THEIR TEACHER

A Practical Resource Guide for *It's Hard to Share My Teacher*

By Joan Singleton Prestine

Fearon Teacher Aids

A Paramount Communications Company

Publisher: Virginia L. Murphy

Editors: Kristin Eclov and Lisa Schwimmer

Illustration: Virginia Kylberg

Cover and Inside Illustration: Virginia Kylberg

Design: Marek/Janci Design

Cover Design: Lucyna Green

Library of Congress Catalog Card Number: 93–74060

ISBN 0-86653-923-9
Printed in the United States of America
1. 9 8 7 6 5 4 3 2 1

Contents

Preface

It is my love of children that drives me to write materials that are insightful about how children think and feel. I want to help children learn, understand, and accept that each one of them is a special and unique individual. As individuals, children bring a variety of experiences with them to school. It can often be difficult for adults to respond to and meet the immediate needs of each child. Sharing a teacher's attention is a learned behavior.

I wrote *Helping Children Share Their Teacher* as a tool for adults to help children find positive responses to the feelings they have when they go to school. Sharing toys can be difficult enough, but sharing a teacher may seem next to impossible for some children. This resource helps adults help children gradually learn how to share—share toys, school supplies, feelings, and eventually, their teacher.

About *It's Hard to Share My Teacher*

The *It's Hard to Share My Teacher* picturebook is designed to help children understand the various feelings and responses they may have when trying to share, including trying to share their teacher. Read the book and discuss the story with children as a prelude to using the activities outlined in this resource.

In the story, Josh discovers it is easier to share the jump rope than to share the jungle gym or the ball. Inside the classroom, Josh learns to share the tables and chairs, the puzzles, and the tambourine. He discovers that it's hard to share the crayons when his favorite colors are gone. Even though he's stuck with yellow, Josh solves his dilemma by drawing bananas. In his excitement to show the bananas to his teacher, Josh becomes disruptive when his teacher seems to ignore him.

When his teacher finally comes over, he tells Josh he likes Josh's bananas and asks Josh to show the group how to draw them. As Josh tries to help the children individually, other children want his attention, too. In his desperation to help all of the children, Josh realizes that he has to share the ball, the jungle gym, the jump rope, the tables, the chairs, the tambourines, the puzzles, the rug, the crayons . . . and the teacher.

Introduction

Children need and want to understand what to share or not to share, when to talk or not to talk, and even how and when to share their teacher. Most young children feel safer with structure in their lives. Communication with the children in your care, as well as communication amongst themselves, is important to you, as well as to the children. Learning to share toys, friends, supplies, feelings, and the teacher's attention takes good communication, as well as a good understanding of other's feelings. Understanding that children are all different, it's sometimes hard to know how they feel or why they respond the way they do.

What works to help a child share his or her teacher today may not work tomorrow, next week, or next month. Yet, with some children, the same methods work over and over. One thing to remember is that children's actions will provoke a feeling within you. You respond to your feelings, so it's important to respond in a way that reinforces positive behavior in the children.

Helping Children Share Their Teacher is a guide to help teachers, parents, and other adults assist children in understanding their feelings and responses about sharing toys, group supplies, and friends, but mostly their feelings and responses about sharing their teacher. This resource guide provides practical suggestions and activities for children to accept responsibility for their responses.

Communication:
A Two-Way Street

Communication between you and each child in your care builds the foundation for each child to have enough trust and security in his or her relationship with you to become independent and responsible enough to share you. By helping children communicate positively with you as well as others, children learn that sharing is a positive thing to do—a way to establish good relationships with those around them.

Literally Speaking

Consider looking at your own communication skills—are the messages you are giving children positive or negative? Think about how children may react to the following statement:

"Sit down and be quiet. Can't you see I'm helping Maria?"

Encourage children to speak and act positively by communicating and modeling positive behavior yourself. The same idea stated in the positive creates more of a desire to cooperate:

"Please sit down and I will help you in a moment. As soon as I finish with Bob, I'll be right over."

Another option might be:

"Please sit down. I want to talk with you. There are three children waiting for me. It will be your turn as soon as I finish with them."

Most children are literal; they believe verbatim what you say. Telling a child he or she is too dependent or hangs on too much places the emphasis on the negative action rather than focusing on the feeling behind the action. In this way, some children inevitably become more dependent.

Chatting with the Children

All children need special time with their teacher. If possible, meet with one or two children individually for a few minutes each day. Keeping a record makes it easy to visit with each child in the group. If you can, continue the visits, giving the children, as well as yourself, the chance for individual connection throughout the year. This special time between you and a child gives you an opportunity to learn more about what's going on in his or her life. It also gives the children a chance to get to know you as well, building a special trust between you. Chat about school, favorite toys, friends, parents, siblings, hobbies, feelings, or visit just for fun. Use this time to build trust and rapport. As children build trust, they are more likely to become independent.

Zap Yes and No Responses

Not all parents encourage their children to talk at home. Some children feel more comfortable with yes and no responses. Prompting children to talk inspires them to think and helps you strengthen your relationships with the children while you learn all about them.

Guide a discussion between you and the children by asking questions, suggesting topics, and encouraging children to delve deeper into how they are feeling. Asking open-ended questions gives children an opportunity to talk and helps them think and answer with a sentence. Start with some of the following open-ended questions:

1. Tell me what you think about . . .
2. I'd like to hear about . . .
3. What do you like to read?
4. Where is your favorite place?
5. If you could go anywhere in the world, where would you go?

The Listening Mirror

You can start to build a strong relationship with a child by really listening to what he or she has to say. Children listen to you, if you listen to them. When a child is telling you something, clarify or summarize the conversation. Repeat back to the child what you heard him or her say and then ask the child if this is correct. Mirror this process with children after you give directions, express your feelings, and so on. Ask the child to clarify or summarize what you said. This mirroring process helps it quickly become clear whether you and the child understand each other.

Children feel their own strength and power when others, especially teachers and adults, ask for their ideas, allow them to express themselves, and then really listen.

Family Crest

Help each child develop and share pride in his or her family through the creation of a family crest. Have each child fold a piece of paper into four sections. In each section, invite the children to draw pictures of their families, pets, favorite toys, books, houses, yards, initials, or names. Build communication skills by encouraging the children to share their crests in detail.

Then have the children share in the fun of creating a class crest. Creation of a class crest makes the class seem more like a family. This way, children learn to communicate as a group when deciding what is important enough to appear on the crest. The colorful crest can be hung in a prominent spot in the room. Individually, children can make their own version of the class crest, first displayed in the room, then shared with their families.

We Need You

Help parents get involved at school by asking them to bring in juice cans, empty milk cartons, food, and other materials necessary for projects. Or, ask parents to volunteer to go on field trips, give interesting presentations to the children, or become an adult helper in the classroom. As you get to know the parents, your opportunities for communication with them will only get better. As the parents see their children at school, children and their parents have more to talk about. Suggest that parents talk with their children about school, what they learned, and what they are interested in. Parental support and input may help children become more independent, but be careful to be sensitive to each child's home environment.

Children's Actions

Some children are calm and quiet, others active and noisy. Some have high self-esteem, others low. Some come from well-adjusted families, receive ample love and attention at home, have rules to follow, others don't.

All children come to school with a different foundation and base of experience. Once at school, they are thrown together and expected to share the same teacher and follow the same rules. For some children, this is easy; for others, it is difficult. It's safe to say that all children respond differently when it comes to sharing their teacher.

Tell Me Why

Why do children act the way they do? "Why" is a big question. Different situations trigger different responses in children. By being aware of many varying factors in children's lives, we, as adults, can help children learn to share their feelings, thoughts, and ideas, as well as school supplies, projects, and their teacher. Keep in mind that some children have a hard time sharing because they:

- have not experienced group play and tend to feel a barrage of unhappy or confused feelings at school.

- have a hard time adjusting to change. Going from an unstructured home environment to a structured school environment is a big change for many children.

- have undivided attention at home and are not used to working in groups.

- can't relate to or don't understand what is being taught.

- learn quickly and become bored when they finish their work.

- have difficulty staying with one activity.

- have low self-esteem.

- receive little attention at home.

- may be yelled at as they leave for school in the morning.

- have a new sibling and don't feel loved.

- are tired because they were awake most of the night with a crying baby, their parents were sick, or children weren't able to sleep because of anxiety.

We can look out for children's feelings by helping them learn to openly express themselves.

Chart Along

Some children learn by listening, others visually, still others learn by doing. Charting children's feelings and how they respond to those feelings involves listening, looking, and doing. Write the following three headings and examples on a chalkboard or on chart paper:

What Happened	How You Feel	What You Do
want teacher's help	sad, mad	talk, cry, wait
grabbed toy	mad, sad, frustrated	hit, tell the teacher

Ask the children to add additional examples.

All About You

Because all children are different, it's important to learn about each child. Send a form home to the family asking about food allergies, other allergies, general health, best foods, worst foods, fears, favorite toys, close friends, neighborhood friends, family status, brothers, sisters, babies on the way, bedtime, rest time, pets, and so on. Any information you learn gives you some understanding about a child's response to sharing, while helping you to get to know the child better.

All About Me

Encourage children to write and illustrate a picturebook about themselves. Invite children to draw pictures about their home life or have them dictate their stories to you. Get the children started with a few questions.

Who lives in your home?
What is your home like?
Where do you sleep?
Who do you share a bedroom with?
Where does your dad work?
Where does your mom work?
Do you have any brothers or sisters?
Where do you play?
What do you do at home?

Do you have pets?
Who do you take care of at home?
Do you have special jobs at home?

Give each child two sheets of construction paper. Invite children to chose any colors they want. Then staple the children's pictures between the construction-paper sheets to make student booklets. Encourage children to decorate their book covers and sign their names.

Sign Up
Meet with each child and talk about one thing he or she would like to learn to do. Work out a contract that you, the child, and the parent all sign. The contract should identify one thing each child would like to learn during the course of the year. With the child and parent, review the contract and update it during the year so everyone can monitor the child's progress.

It's important for you, the children, and the parents to establish a relationship as soon as possible. The more communication among the three of you, the more you and the parents can work together to help the children learn to share their teacher, reinforce skills learned at school, and help children reach their goals. A contract is a perfect way to expand these lines of communication.

What to Do: How Activities Help

Activities are an excellent way of encouraging children to share in positive and constructive ways. The practical activities in this resource guide help children understand many aspects of sharing and why sharing is important. They reassure children that it is normal to sometimes have difficulty learning to share. When possible, encourage active participation from all children. Children often learn best through hands-on activities. The activities in this resource are not intended to address children who may have severe emotional or adjustment problems. These children may need to receive special professional guidance.

Suggestions for Implementing the Activities

- Don't tell children how to feel or react. Like adults, children need to express their own feelings. Give basic directions, but allow children freedom to create their own projects with little outside interference. Their projects will be more meaningful to them if children create according to their own rules in a loosely structured environment.
- Provide a play environment in which activities can be introduced. This type of environment encourages children to approach feelings and thoughts that might otherwise be too uncomfortable to deal with.
- Some children choose to engage in one activity over and over and not to participate in others. That's okay. An activity may be perfect for one child and not useful for another. Feel free to rotate activities depending on the needs of the children.
- The thoughts and feelings children experience while participating in a project are important considerations. Encourage children to verbalize how they are feeling while participating.

The activities that follow explore how children feel about sharing as presented in the children's book *It's Hard to Share My Teacher*. After listening to the children's comments and questions and helping them express how they feel, choose activities that are appropriate to meet each child's particular emotional needs.

Sharing Toys

**"I'm learning to share the crayons.
But sharing crayons can be hard. I like
coloring with red and blue.
But sometimes there's only yellow."**

These words from the book *It's Hard to Share My Teacher* show that Josh is learning to share.

By pointing out the advantages of sharing, children become more willing and even excited about sharing. Explain to children that there are times when sharing can be difficult for everyone, even adults.

Do As I Do

Children's behavior is influenced by the interactions they observe on a day-to-day basis. Therefore, it's easier to teach children about sharing when they are consistently exposed to respectful and considerate behavior. Create an environment in which everyone is treated with kindness and respect. For example, use the word "share" when you talk with the children. Encourage the children to share their thoughts, opinions, and ideas. Explain how it feels to share and why you like to share. Comment if you see children showing sharing behaviors, such as kindness, respect, and consideration.

> "My mom made lots of cookies, so I brought some to share."
> "Scott, will you share your crayons with me? Thanks. I like it when you share with me."
> "I feel like being your friend."

Share Chair

Children usually have favorite toys they want to show their friends, but not really share with them. Having a "share chair" allows a child to show his or her special toy to the other children without letting them handle it. Encourage toy owners to also share special information about their toys with the group. After the toys are shared, have children put their toys in their cubby holes or in your cabinet for safe-keeping.

Grab Bag

Ask the children to bring small inexpensive objects from home. Place all the items in a bag and ask each child to choose one object. Encourage the children to keep or trade the items they picked out of the bag. Encourage the children to share their feelings about trading their objects for other children's objects. After everyone has settled on an item, encourage the children to show their objects to the group.

Share Corner

Suggest that children bring an object from home to leave at school for one week. Set up a special corner to display the items. Remind the children to be careful when handling the objects on display. For some children, it will be difficult to leave their items at school. Help the children understand that their items still belong to them, but by leaving the objects at school, they are sharing them with everyone for a short time. Seeing the other children enjoying their treasures often gives the owners a feeling of pride, yet an understanding that they can share objects without losing ownership.

If a child refuses to share, for whatever reason, respect his or her feelings. A child should never be forced to share. Offer the child other options to participate in sharing when he or she feels ready.

Clock In

There are always favorite toys that children have a difficult time sharing. Unfortunately, these are often the same toys that everyone wants to play with. As a group, decide on a fair length of time for each child to play with the most popular toys in the classroom. Use an egg timer to monitor the children's playtime. When the timer goes off, it is time for a new child to play with the toy. The egg timer is a helpful tool in teaching children how to move from one activity to the next. As the children become comfortable with a monitored playtime, they are learning to share toys as well as time in the classroom.

Sharing Group Supplies

**"I'm learning to share the tables and chairs,
the tambourines, and the puzzles. I like
sharing the puzzles because two can put
a puzzle together faster than one."**

These words from the book *It's Hard to Share My Teacher*
show Josh is learning to share group supplies.

Learning how to share is a process that takes place over
time. Children do not automatically know how to share,
therefore they need to be given opportunities to learn. It's
not unusual for children to react to a new sharing situation
negatively because they are uncertain about how to react.
Give children a clear understanding that they don't have to
share some things, like their cubby holes, and they do need
to share other things, like tambourines.

Now Is the Time

Children are more secure knowing how their group functions, when they will work alone, and when they will work with the teacher. Children need to know what supplies to share and when to share them. When appropriate, write a brief schedule of activities on the chalkboard. Older children can help by writing the schedule for you. As children learn to follow the routine, they also learn what supplies are needed for each activity. Rotating monitors can pass out the supplies and put them away.

Our Puppets

Ask the children to help collect some of the supplies for the group to make puppets. Have the children bring clean, old socks from home. Beans are perfect for stuffing the socks. Buttons are great for eyes and use markers to make the mouths. For younger children, use old nylon stockings for stuffing the puppets and use markers to draw facial features.

After the children finish their puppets, it's time for a puppet show! For the first production, have the children use the puppets they made. For the second show, recommend that the children trade puppets. Explain to the children that they are going to share their puppets with the group. Have each child put his or her puppet on a table. Have all the children stand in a circle behind their puppets. Ask the children to walk past three puppets. Explain that the fourth puppet is the puppet they'll use for the next show. After the show, invite children to return the puppets to the children who made them.

Togetherness

Divide the group into smaller groups of two or three children. Encourage each group to choose an activity that they can all do together, such as creating a story, making a mural, and so on. Explain that it is important that all the children in each group decide on the activity and the supplies needed to participate in that activity. After the children are finished with their activities, encourage them to share their experiences with the other groups.

Musical Chairs

Some children get into the habit of sitting in the same spots for snack and lunchtime. Play a song on a tape recorder. Invite the children to march around the table until the music stops and then sit on the chair in front of them. This activity helps keep children from becoming possessive of an area and encourages feeling comfortable with change.

Rotation

Occasionally children love doing one particular activity over and over and tend to ignore other activities and supplies. With each child, make an individual chart of all the activities and supplies offered. Help each child understand that he or she can do a favorite activity once and then he or she should try two other activities before returning to the favorite one again. If a child is uninterested in an activity, that's okay. Respect the child's choice. Help the child keep track of his or her own activities using different-colored crayons or stickers. The children can take their charts home to share what they have been doing with their families.

Sharing Friends

**"I'm learning to share the
jungle gym and the jump rope, too.
Sometimes sharing can be fun."**

These words from the book *It's Hard to Share My Teacher* show the importance of friends and sharing.

Friends are important to most school-age children. Some children will do almost anything to gain acceptance by their peers. Others are more standoffish. It's important for all children to feel as though they have friends. Often it's harder to share friends than toys.

Let's Be Friends

Talk with the children about what they think makes a good friend. Record the children's ideas on the chalkboard. Share with the group the qualities you look for in a good friend as well, such as someone who is kind and a good listener.

Encourage the children to practice being good friends. Divide the group into pairs. Give each pair of children a "sharing" assignment, such as saying a nice thing to their partner, helping their partner with a project, or playing a game together. Then have the pairs of children rotate. Not only will the children get to know each other better, but they will also learn sharing through their "sharing" assignments.

Me Against Me

Instead of encouraging competition between the children, encourage the children to do their best in everything they do. Stress the importance of children doing their best in order to feel good about themselves. Share words of praise with each child who makes an effort to participate in each activity. Encourage the children to help each other and give each other praise.

Small Groups

It can be hard for children to make new friends. Encourage the children to make new friends by dividing the class into smaller groups of four children. Try arranging the groups randomly or possibly by common interests. Encourage the small groups to work together on a project, such as rearranging the blocks, making a new poster for Earth Day, or setting up for snacktime. Invite the children to share their small-group experiences with the rest of the class.

I'm Sorry, So Sorry

An apology needs to be sincere. Forcing a child to apologize when he or she doesn't mean it teaches that child to be less than truthful. It is important to realize that sometimes children are not really sorry about something they've done and you need to accept that. Encourage the children to share their feelings about intentionally or unintentionally hurting someone. Help the children understand that it is possible to hurt someone physically as well as hurt someone's feelings. Invite the children to share their experiences with being hurt and how they felt afterwards.

My Time

Friends are important, but there are times when children may want time to be alone or play quietly. Create a special corner of the classroom that can be used as a quiet corner. Encourage the children to share their thoughts and feelings about daily events in personal journals. Younger children can use pictures and older children can record their thoughts in writing. Invite the children to use the quiet corner for journaling.

Sharing Feelings

"'Mr. Gilbert? Look what I drew with yellow.'"

"'Mr. Gilbert?'"

"Mr. Gilbert is busy helping Matthew."

These words from the book *It's Hard to Share My Teacher* show Josh's initial feelings of frustration because he doesn't feel his teacher is listening to him.

Most teachers would not knowingly ignore a child's feelings. But hurt feelings can occur unintentionally. Both adults and children need to accept that no one is perfect—that most people try to do their best.

Learning to share feelings is vital to a child's emotional growth. Teach the children that part of sharing is learning to share their feelings, as well as sharing things, time, or people. By sharing their feelings in healthy ways, children learn that to give of themselves not only helps them, but also helps others to understand them. This, too, is an important part of sharing.

Many young children do not always clearly understand that they have choices about their responses to their feelings. We, as adults, can teach children how to respond to their feelings in healthy ways.

Feelings of the Day

Use a few minutes each day to share the many different feelings the children have recently experienced. Share individually, in small groups, or with the whole class. Ask the children to talk about what happened to bring on the feelings and how they responded to them. Share with the children some of your feelings as well. Reassure children that it is okay to feel the way they do. The more children think about what happened to cause the feelings, and how they responded to the feelings, the more likely they will think before they respond to feelings and not simply react.

Feeling Faces

Invite the children to help you list a variety of different feelings on the chalkboard—happy, jealous, impatient, selfish, angry, scared, sad, cranky, lonely, frustrated, ashamed, shy, left out, or tired. Talk about what the feelings mean. It's difficult for some children to put feelings into words or to express their feelings constructively. Give each child several paper plates. Ask the children to draw faces on their plates that represent several of the feelings listed on the board. Help the children write the name of the feeling underneath each drawing. Make a hole in the top of each child's assortment of paper-plate faces. Help the children string their plates onto a piece of yarn.

Ask the children to hang the plates on the back of their chairs, on hooks, or in front of their cubby holes. As children's feelings change throughout the day, encourage them to flip their plate faces to show how they feel at the moment. Then encourage the children to share their feelings verbally.

Stressed Out

Emotional stress in children can be as common as stress in adults. It is important to recognize when a child is under stress. Most children under stress experience a change in behavior. This behavior can often be disruptive or withdrawn. If appropriate, encourage a child who shows signs of stress to share his or her feelings or the source of the stress with you. Be respectful and supportive if a child chooses not to share his or her feelings with you. Help the child find ways to alleviate some of the stress.

Exercise is an important ingredient to combat stress and promote healthy bodies and minds. Invite children to play non-competitive games outside. Competitive games often increase stress. Encourage children to ride bikes, play tag, or do gymnastics to reduce stress. Encourage children to share in games with other children. Sharing games together can help reduce stress in both children and adults.

The Angry Me

It is unhealthy for both adults and children to hold in their anger. Encourage children to vent their anger in a constructive, safe manner, but try not to encourage aggressive behavior. If children have pent-up energy and disrupt others, encourage them to run laps outside or engage in other physical activity. Be sure that children understand that exercise is not a punishment for their feelings. If children can't verbalize their feelings constructively, encourage them to create with clay or paint. Ask the children for additional ideas to work off anger.

When a child appears angry and can't verbalize the feeling, take out a piece of paper and crayons. Invite the child to draw what happened to cause the anger. While drawing, encourage the child to talk about his or her picture. Invite the child to share how he or she could appropriately respond to the angry feelings.

The Frustrated Me

Everyone feels frustrated at times. A child who has difficulty with reading or with numbers may feel continual frustration. This frustration may show up every time reading or math is taught. It is important the children feel comfortable enough to share their feelings of frustration with you or other classmates. Encourage children to ask questions if they don't understand something. Sharing frustrations with friends often helps alleviate the stress.

Some children cope better with frustrating activities after a short break. Other times, encouraging a frustrated child to ask a friend for help also works well. A frustrated child may be more receptive to suggestions from a friend. This promotes sharing and communication among the children.

The Happy Me

Children who feel good about themselves and have high self-esteem seem to adjust well in school and usually don't have a major problem sharing their teacher. One way to boost self-esteem is to have a reward system using a monthly theme. For example, the theme for January could be winter. Show the children how to cut out white snow people and glue them onto blue construction paper. Display everyone's snow person on a bulletin board. Help children use a hole punch to cut out circles from white construction paper. When a child shares with another, such as sharing supplies or toys, give that child a white snowflake circle to glue onto his or her picture. Reward each child for participating and doing his or her best. Many snowflakes can be rewarded for effort. At the end of the month, suggest the children take their pictures home to share with their families.

Following is a list of months followed by a suggested theme, project, and reward:

Month	Theme	Project	Reward
January	winter	snow people	white circles
February	friendship	red hearts	candy hearts
March	solar system	black paper	moon and stars
April	weather	clouds	raindrops
May	spring	flowers	petals
June	vegetable garden	corn	corn kernels
July	beach	beach balls	dots on beach balls
August	summer	apple trees	apples
September	fall	trees	leaves on the ground
October	Halloween	pumpkins	pumpkin seeds
November	harvest	baskets	vegetables in basket
December	holidays	houses	holiday lights

The Jealous Me

There are many reasons for a child to feel jealous. There may be more behind a child's feelings of jealousy in sharing. For example, a new sibling can often cause an older child to react more strongly to certain situations. Sharing attention from his or her parents can be very difficult for a child. Encourage the child to share his or her feelings with you or a friend. If appropriate, invite other children who have younger sisters and brothers to talk about how they felt when a new member joined their families. Discuss how important big brothers and big sisters are to their baby brothers and sisters. Encourage the children to share their experiences with the group.

Suggest that the child with the new sibling choose one or two friends to help put on a play about the new baby. The child may be able to work through some of his or her feelings through role playing. You may want to note which role the child chooses to play—mom, dad, another sibling, himself or herself, or the baby. Watch how the child relates to the other members of the family.

The Sad Me

Some children feel insecure, almost as if they don't belong. Instead of trying to fit in, some children mentally withdraw from the other children or from the teacher.

Children who are insecure may need special attention. This attention may be as simple as reading a child a story about someone who is insecure or sad. The story may offer the child some comfort or solutions to his or her own troubles. Hopefully you can gently draw the child out. The child may be more comfortable talking to you through a puppet, stuffed animal, or using a flannel storyboard. Never force a child to participate in this activity if he or she doesn't want to. Offer the child options to participate when he or she feels ready.

The Scared Me
Don't underestimate the power of children's fear. Fear affects behavior and the ability to learn. Children can be afraid for their physical safety. For example, some children are afraid of the playground slide, another child, or even a pair of scissors. Emotional fear is very real to children. It is important to demonstrate respect for children by acknowledging their fears. For example, some children are afraid they won't know the answer to a question and other children will call them stupid, that their teacher may criticize them, or that their peers might laugh at them and they won't have any friends.

Acknowledging a fear is an important step toward overcoming it. Suggest that children draw pictures of actions or situations that frighten them. Then have each child make up a story to go along with what frightens him or her. Invite discussion. Share some of your own fears with the children as well to begin the discussion. Sometimes knowing that others share the same fears, too, helps to alleviate the children's own fears. Encourage the children to talk about how they respond to their fears. Having a child draw a picture, make up a story, then share the story with you, a small group, or the whole class, puts that child in control of his or her fear. By sharing his or her fear with the class, the power of the fear can diminish for the child.

The Shy Me

It may be difficult for a shy child to share, only because he or she is too shy to reach out to others. Encourage a shy child to pursue an interest, such as drawing or painting. Display the child's artwork for all to see. Praise the child for participating in the activity. Try to include all the children in activities when they are interested.

Find a picturebook and encourage a shy child to tell you the story from the pictures. In the beginning, the child may be willing to only talk to you. Find different picturebooks and gradually add children to the group, until the child is sharing a story with the whole class.

Sharing the Teacher

"Mr. Gilbert is always busy with the other children. I'm starting to feel impatient. I think I'll play with Scott instead."

These words from the book *It's Hard to Share My Teacher* show how important it is for Josh to learn to be more patient.

The relationship between young children and their teacher is of primary concern to them. A young child may have strong emotional ties with the teacher and mainly want interaction only with the teacher. As a child becomes older, the teacher becomes less of a central figure in the child's life. Instead of looking to the teacher for approval, children begin to look to their friends for approval.

Children have many friends, but only one teacher. Like a parent, a teacher plays a major role in a child's future. Children learn how to act and react from watching how parents and teachers interact with others. Children need to feel they are special. Encourage respectful and supportive behavior towards children.

Warm Fuzzies
Building trust with the children helps them share the teacher and become more comfortable working and playing independently. Try to develop something special between you and each child in the classroom. This can be a project you work on together, a book you both enjoy, a common hobby, or a caring conversation. That way, each child feels as if he or she is important and that they always have something special to do with you or to talk with you about. This helps the children build self-confidence. The relationship between the teacher or adult and the child should be one of trust. Encourage children to do their best and to always try. Praise a child's efforts as well as successes.

Notes from You to Me
To help children build a more mature relationship with you (so they are willing to share you), treat children with kindness and respect. Respect children's opinions. Listen to their comments and suggestions. Create an environment where communication is open and encouraged. Ask children to write you notes about their feelings toward school, what they like and dislike about school, what they would change, and how they would change it. Ask children to sign their names so you can respond to their notes. Have a mailbox for the children to place their notes. Children too young to write can verbalize their thoughts to you. Notes and comments to the teacher are a way for the children to feel they have some control over what's going on in school.

Take Ten
Set aside ten minutes each day to help a child choose and lead a game, such as "Simon Says." Provide specific guidelines for the child to follow. Then encourage the child to call

the group together and direct the activity. This activity helps to develop communication between you and the child, teaches decision-making, and builds leadership skills. As children become more confident, they become more independent and won't rely on you as much. Strongly suggest that all children, even the shy or quiet ones, participate at least once every couple of months.

Wish List

Sharing a teacher is hard work for many children. Some children cope better in smaller groups. Work in large and small groups to encourage sharing. It's important to let the children know that there are days when "I wish there were 20 of me, so there would be one of me for each one of you." Then ask the children what their special wish for school would be. Place a large piece of butcher paper on the floor. Invite the children to use crayons or markers to draw pictures of their school wishes. Children can dictate sentences to go with their pictures. Then display the "wish list" on a wall.

Changing the Mood

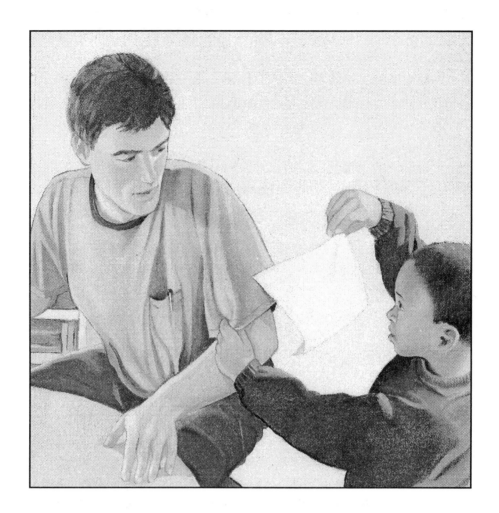

**"'I'll be with you in a minute, Josh. Please sit
down and work on your picture.'"**

These words from the book *It's Hard to Share My Teacher*
show Mr. Gilbert's patience with Josh, even as Josh is tug-
ging on his shirt.

The mood of the classroom often affects how the classroom operates. If you are frustrated, upset, or impatient, that
mood can easily carry over to the children in your care
—and visa versa. Change the mood of the classroom by
inviting children to participate in setting the classroom
atmosphere. Children can help with class schedules, snacktime, rules, playtime, and so on. This not only gives children
a sense of responsibility, but also sets a mood for communication and sharing among you and the children.

Be Your Best

Groups function at their best when there are guidelines that are consistently followed. Set guidelines with the children that they can understand and want to follow. Ask each child to come up with one rule for the classroom. When the list is complete, ask the entire group to participate in making a colorful poster listing new class guidelines. Encourage children to choose a highly visible wall to display the poster.

Encourage the use of respectful and considerate behavior. Model the kind of behavior you want the children to use. Setting limits for behavior allows everyone to share the teacher's time. Children will have a stronger sense of self-esteem and achieve more success because they will know what behavior is expected of them.

Encourage Flexibility

Schedules are a necessity. Helping children adjust to change is also a necessity. Instill a positive response to change in the children by being flexible with the group. Flexibility doesn't mean giving up structure, control, and guidelines. For example, to change the mood of your classroom, periodically rearrange the room with the help of the children. Ask children for ideas on how to change the room decor. Rotate seats, change jobs, teams, and team captains regularly. The more flexible children are, the more comfortable they are with change. By teaching the children to be flexible in changing seats, schedules, and activities, they are learning to share and be less possessive.

My Progress

Encourage each child to share how his or her day is progressing. Encourage the children to share their experiences with classmates, parents, and the teacher. If one day is bad, talk about how the next day can be improved. Encourage the children to share what they think can be changed to make the next day better. Have children draw pictures of events, good or bad, that they want to share with you or their families.

Learning Positive Expression

**"I'm learning to share the ball, even though
I don't always want to."**

These words from the book *It's Hard to Share My Teacher*
show that Josh is still having some trouble sharing—but he's
trying.

One of the most important things you can do for children
is to help them respond positively to feelings of anger or
frustration. These feelings can impede a child's ability or
desire to share the teacher's attention. By learning to
respond positively to these feelings, a child can become
more receptive to sharing the teacher. Together, set guidelines that let children know when and how to respond to
their feelings of frustration and anger. Encourage children to

show respect for each other. Help children learn to express their emotions in constructive and positive ways.

Instant Replay

It's helpful for children to understand what kinds of actions trigger feelings that make them feel like acting out physically. If children don't understand their feelings, they will probably respond in much the same way each time a feeling is experienced or triggered. Encourage children to share the kinds of things that make them angry and why. Discuss other ways to deal with anger that are nonviolent. Then help the children talk about how they can respond more positively if such a feeling happens again. Use the "Chart Along" activity on page 16 to help children list some positive responses.

Puttin' on the Ritz

Invite children to dramatize stories, plays, and poems—or encourage the children to think of their own stories for dramatic play. Send a note home with children asking parents to donate clothing, old dishes, books, and other materials for the children to use as props. Store the materials in marked boxes, such as "clothing," "kitchen materials," " hats," and so on. Divide the class into small groups and help each group brainstorm how to present their skits. Not only will the children be sharing ideas, they will also be sharing costumes and props, as well as the teacher's attention. Challenge children to use their imaginations in dramatizing the stories.

Feelings Journal

Some children may not be able to or want to verbalize their feelings with you. Invite children to write down or draw pictures of their feelings in a journal. Encourage children to choose any way of expressing themselves in their journals as they wish. Children may share their journal entries if they want to, or they can keep their journals private. Either way, the journals are a good outlet for their feelings. Give children two sheets of construction paper and some writing or drawing paper. Use a three-hole punch to punch holes along one side of each of the pages. Children can put their journal pages in notebooks or you can provide them with small rings to hold their pages together. Children can add to their journals as they need to.

Expressing Anger and Frustration

Children who act out physically towards other children need to learn other ways to express their feelings. Give the child a ball to kick, if you feel this is necessary. This activity can be used when a child needs a more constructive outlet for anger, frustration, and so on. Encourage kicking a ball against an outside wall, hitting a volleyball, or punching a pillow. Help children talk about what makes them angry. Sometimes, after children have worked off their feelings physically, they are more able to express themselves verbally about how they feel.

Super Kid

If you see a child lashing out at another physically, this may be a way to get your attention. Though you do not approve of this behavior, the child obviously has a need— you. Discuss with the child what he or she is feeling. Give that child some of your attention. Then compliment the child on things he or she has handled well. Make the time together positive.

Specifically complimenting children for being attentive while you read a book, or quietly waiting while you are on the phone or finishing a project, gives children more positive feelings about themselves. Write children's names on the chalkboard and put checks next to their names as they receive more compliments. Model the types of interactions and behaviors you want children to develop. Praise each child for participating or trying to accomplish a task. Use checks by children's names for participation and effort as well. It's important for children to feel good about doing their best.

Making a Mural

Encourage children to express themselves through art. Invite children to make a mural together. Using a long sheet of butcher paper, children can make a mural of activities they would like to share with friends. Some suggestions could be sharing games, swimming, playing basketball, jacks, sharing stories, snacks, and so on.

Bulletin-Board Art

Invite children to decorate a bulletin board as a group. Ask children to give you theme ideas for the bulletin board, such as seasons, holidays, or even feelings. Making an "impatient" bulletin board may give children the opportunity to express their feelings of impatience with words, in a story or poem, or in pictures. Use different themes, encourage children to share their ideas with one another, help each other out with their contributions to the board, and so on. This is a good "sharing of ideas" activity.

Group Story

Anther good "sharing of ideas" activity is to invite children to tell a story together. Have children sit with you in a circle on the floor. Explain to the children that you are going to begin a story and you want them to help you finish it. Start the story and then go around the circle, asking each child to contribute a sentence or two. If possible, write down what the children say as you go around the circle. Read the story in its entirety after it is finished and share with the children.

Sharing Attention

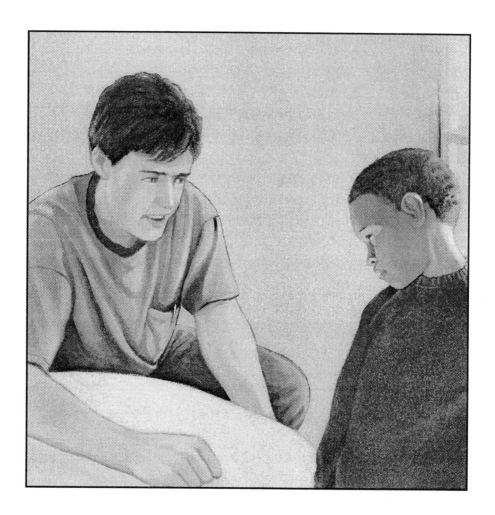

**"'Josh, it's hard for me to help the other children
when you and Scott are noisy.'"**

**"'But I want to show you my picture.
And you won't help me.'"**

These words from the book *It's Hard to Share My Teacher*
show Josh's trouble understanding why his teacher won't
immediately give him his full attention.

A child's feelings may be hurt or a child may even feel that
the teacher doesn't care about him or her when the teacher
is not immediately available. It's important for children to
learn that the teacher cares about them, but can't always
give his or her undivided attention to each child when that

child wants or needs it. Children can learn patience and understanding.

Speaking softly to a group of children helps children learn to listen. The more quietly you speak, the more intently children need to listen in order to hear you. Soon the children get into the habit of quietly listening when you speak.

Talk Time

Some children just need time to talk. "Talk time" gives children legitimate floor time to talk. You may want to have "talk time" first thing in the morning to give everyone a chance to share with you and the rest of the group the exciting events of the day before. Some children are more verbal than others, so you may want to use a timer. Others may need to be coaxed to talk at all. Encourage the children to talk about whatever they want, or you can suggest themes—favorite toys, books, clothing, exciting events, and so on.

Newsletter Reporters

As a group, help the children create a newsletter to share with their families. A regular newsletter from the children keeps parents informed about what the children are learning and how their group is functioning. Parents can then reinforce new skills learned in school and get involved in what their children are doing.

Encourage children to write sentences or draw illustrations for the newsletter. Keep children's contributions simple and age-appropriate. Encourage children to share stories, information, announcements, and so on in the newsletter. If children have ideas or comments, encourage children to list them.

Sharing Words

Invite children to share kind words with each other. Ask children to help you make a list of positive words on the chalkboard or on chart paper. Encourage children to talk about when and to whom they use those words. Invite children to draw pictures, write, or dictate sentences about being kind. Display the children's work in the room or invite children to take their kind word pictures home to share with their families.

Share My Teacher

Invite the children to act out the story of *It's Hard to Share My Teacher*. Divide the group into smaller groups. Help each group decide who will be each character in the story. Encourage sharing by suggesting to the children that they take turns being the primary characters. Have the groups practice their role-playing and then invite each group to present the story. Invite creativity in their presentations.

How to Encourage Sharing Time and Space--Taking Turns

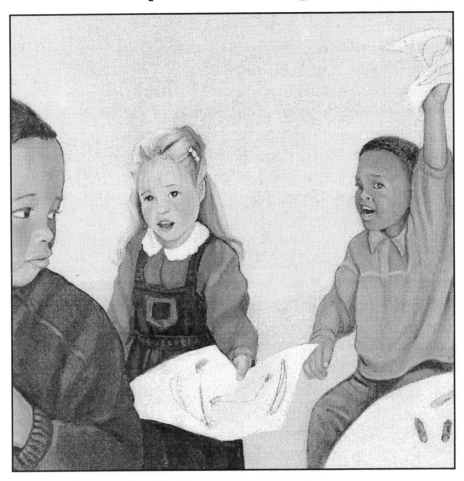

"'Josh, come here and help me.'"

"'No, Josh, help me! I had my hand up first!'"

These words from the book *It's Hard to Share My Teacher* show how the children in the story all want Josh's attention.

Often children feel ignored. Children sometimes use whatever tactic seems to work to get someone to pay attention to them. Learning to share space and time with others helps children learn about boundaries as well as sharing with their friends. Children need their own space, just like adults do—they need to have their own space, for play, thinking, and so on. Help children learn to share not only their belongings, but their time, space, and themselves.

Puppet Leaders

Sharing someone's attention is a hard concept. Consistently model the kind of habits and interactions you want children to develop. Children respond well to puppets. Use a puppet to give the children directions—go to the rug to hear a story, pick up toys, or take out their papers. You could use a different puppet to announce each activity. The children often know what to do as soon as they see the puppet.

Traveling Treasures

Recommend that children bring special objects to school to share. Bring in something special yourself. Invite children to take turns sharing their treasures during circle time. Children may even want to share their treasures throughout the day. If they choose not to share during the day, explain to children that that's okay. Encourage children to also share why their treasures are special.

Family Bulletin Board

Ask the children to bring in some family photos. Bring in photos of your family as well. Help children hang the photos at eye level on the bulletin board. Have the children introduce their families to the group and tell what they like to do with their families. Encourage children to share information about their families as well, such as information about their pets, family trips, special family traditions, and so on. Give each child a turn to share.

School Family

Stuffed animals or puppets from school can become a child's school family. Suggest that a child adopt a group of animals or puppets, maybe the same number as in his or her real family. Encourage the child to put on a show with his or her school family.

Sharing Time

Encourage "sharing time." Help children feel more comfortable with sharing their feelings. "Sharing time" helps children learn to communicate with their teacher and friends while everyone is together, instead of one to one. Becoming comfortable speaking in front of a group is easy for some children and hard for others.

Yonder Table

Move chairs or desks around in the room to help children learn to share their space—tables, seats in reading groups, lines, and so on. Praise children for their ability to share space. Work out a schedule where children can sit in a different place throughout the week. Invite children to come up with other ways to share the room space, such as play space, personal space, small group space, and so on. Then give each child a piece of construction paper and invite the children to make special signs for each space. Display the signs to label the room spaces.

Book Time

Encourage children to share favorite books with friends or the whole group. If children are too young to read, they can tell the story from the pictures. It's not unusual for some children to be uncomfortable speaking in front of a group, but, through time, their self-confidence should increase. Never force a child to participate if he or she doesn't want to.

Comedy Production

Encourage creative play and a variety of choices. Invite children to use their creative talents in group skits. Divide the group into smaller groups. Give each group a skit topic, such as stories they have read together, act out a joke, and so on. Or, encourage children to come up with their own ideas for skits. Comedy is a good stress reliever and this activity encourages sharing time and ideas.

Stand-Up Comedian

Instead of just sharing jokes with you or a few of their friends, once a week invite anyone who wants to share a joke with the group to do so. Some children may want to do funny sounds, facial expressions, or body movements.

Student Tutoring

Encourage student tutoring as a way for children to learn to share their time, as well as giving help to others. Not only will a child receive help, but the child tutoring is sharing of herself or himself. This also allows you to help the children who may be having more difficult problems. This way, children are sharing time with you!

Building Self-Esteem

**"'I can help you now, Josh. This is a
very nice picture.'"**

These words from the book *It's Hard to Share My Teacher*
show Mr. Gilbert's praise for Josh's artwork.

It's often difficult to build a child's self-esteem, yet easy for
self-esteem to crumble. Children are very sensitive to hurtful
comments. Low self-esteem may lead to low productivity,
peer conflicts, absenteeism, tardiness, lying, and an "I don't
care" attitude. High self-esteem helps children respond pro-
ductively in a group environment. Good self-esteem is a big
part of being able to share or give of oneself.

Catch a Kid

Nothing does more for self-esteem than catching children doing something positive and then rewarding them for their efforts. Work out a reward system for the children. When you see a child doing something positive, reward the child. You can catch kids helping others, taking on responsibility, participating in projects, making an effort, and so on. When a child feels good about herself or himself, sharing comes more easily.

Best Helpers

Most children enjoy helping others. It makes them feel important, valued, and needed. Helping builds the self-esteem of the child giving the help and provides one-on-one attention to a child who needs extra help. Children begin to realize that someone besides their teacher can help them, too. Encourage helping each other in the classroom. Children can help others clean up, work on projects, tutor, and so on. Create a help chart to display in the classroom. List each child's name on the left-hand side and leave spaces to fill in. When a child is helpful to you or others, make a note of it on the chart. Reward children for trying, as well as participating.

Grab a Compliment

Have each child decorate a box for special notes. When you see a child share a toy, read quietly, walk down the hall, or share a task, write a compliment on a piece of paper and put it into the child's box. You or the child can read the compliment aloud. When all of the compliments have been read, the box is ready to go home with the child to be shared with the family, if he or she wishes.

Sharing Yourself

Sometimes sharing with others can make children feel very good about themselves. Contact a local food distribution center and set up a time when you can bring in donated items. Invite children to bring in canned and boxed foods to share with the food shelf. Have a collection box in the room and, if possible, have the children go with you to the food shelf to share the food they brought from home.

Or, hold a bake sale to raise money for a cause chosen by the children. Explain to the children that many organizations need money to help others. Ask the children what organizations or causes they would like to raise money for, such as a homeless shelter, protecting the rain forest, American Cancer Society, and so on. Send a letter home to parents asking them to donate baked goods for your bake sale. After the money has been raised, invite the children to help you write a letter to the chosen organization to accompany the donation. Encourage each child to "sign" the letter.

Tell Us About You

Give children a chance to share the heritage, culture, and traditions of their families. Set aside time for children to bring something from home that is special about their families or culture. Children can bring in foods that are traditional in their families, clothing, stories, and so on. You may want to invite parents to come in and talk about their backgrounds and traditions as well. Sponsor a "Cultural Day" where everyone can bring something from home that signifies the specialness of each of their families.

Sharing Responsibility

**"'Do you want to show the other children how
you drew with yellow?'"**

"'Yes, please.'"

These words from the book *It's Hard to Share My Teacher*
show how much Josh wants to share with his classmates.

Children are never too young to be leaders or to learn to
speak in front of a group. Even children who seem to
depend heavily on their teacher can be encouraged to share
responsibility.

Group Work
One way to encourage children to become independent is
to suggest they unite as a group. They could consider their

group a club and choose a mascot, design and make a flag, write a song, choose colors, and even have a name. Help the children decide how many club officers they need. Make sure each child has an opportunity to hold each office. Encourage children to develop leadership and speaking skills by talking in front of the group. Let the children use their creativity to plan themes for parties and decide on refreshments and activities.

Sharing Responsibilities

Make a job jar. Ask the children to help you make a list of all the things that need to be done in the classroom. A few examples are:

line leader	calendar monitor
plant monitor	paper passer
wastebasket emptier	circle-time helper
weather monitor	recess helper
snacktime helper	snacktime cleanup
sweeper	toy monitor

Write the names of each job on a slip of paper and place the slips in a jar big enough for a child's hand to pass through. Invite each child to pull a slip of paper from the jar. Or, ask children to volunteer for the jobs. After a week, have children choose again, taking turns at each job.

You Can Teach, Too

Play-acting helps children understand what it's like to be the teacher. Encourage children to move chairs around to construct a group setting in which they can be the teacher. Have the children take turns teaching. Children can teach the others how to build a house with blocks, teach a particular song or poem, or anything the child would like to do. Discuss with the children how they felt as they were teaching.

Take One

Help the children take turns being the teacher by taking on one responsibility. Have each child be in charge of an activity: Pledge of Allegiance, national anthem, lining up for recess, storytime, art, or snacktime. Encourage children to give directions, speak clearly and loudly, and help the others follow directions. After each child has had a chance to lead an activity, start a discussion. How did he or she feel about teaching? What did he or she like to teach? Did the other children listen to them?

First You, Then Me

Create enough responsibilities so that there is a leadership position or position of responsibility for each child in the classroom. Divide the number of jobs by the number of weeks. Rotate jobs so each child has an opportunity to hold each position. Paper passer, plant waterer, snacktime helper, trash collector, door holder, line leader, lunch monitors, officers, team captains—everyone rotates positions.

Additional Resources

Chandler, Louis A. Children Under Stress. Springfield, IL: Thomas, 1985.
  This book gives teachers, caregivers, and parents a resource on understanding the emotional adjustment and reactions to stress of children in their care.

Dodge, Diane Trister and Laura J. Colker. Creative Curriculum for Early Childhood. Washington: Teaching Strategies, Inc., 1992.
  This resource provides information on various curriculum subjects for early-childhood teachers. The book emphasizes changing and enriching the classroom environment to support learning and creativity in children.

Miller, Karen. Ages and Stages. Chelsea, MA: Telshare Publishing Co., 1985.

This book discusses various developmental stages children go through from birth to age eight. Includes developmental descriptions, activities, information on sensory stimulation, and more.

Mitchell, Anne and Judy David. Exploration with Young Children. The Bank Street College of Education. Mt. Ranier, MD: Gryphon House, 1992.

Combining research, practice, publishing, and outreach, Bank Street is now composed of the Graduate School of Education, a model school for children and a family center, and a research division. Through the efforts of all of these divisions, Bank Street works to improve the education of young children by preparing teachers, demonstrating their approach, conducting research, and creating materials for teachers, children, and parents.

Naylor, Phyllis Reynolds. Getting Along with Your Friends. Nashville, TN: Abingdon, 1980.

A self-help approach to making and getting along with friends, exploring the purpose of friendship, understanding the feelings and behavior of oneself and others, and changing one's behavior.

Books for Children

   Good children's books are excellent for stimulating conversation about feelings and emotions. Children, regardless of age, will usually respond by listening, thinking, imagining, and then expressing their thoughts. Reading a book about a similar experience that a child is facing can help him or her vicariously work through and solve his or her own problems. Reading helps children realize they are not alone.

   The following is an annotated bibliography of some quality literature selections dealing with sharing that are appropriate for preschool to third-grade children. Choose the books that best suit the needs of the children in your care.

The Bear's Water Picnic

by John Yeoman
New York: Atheneum, 1987

The pig, squirrel, hedgehog, and hen join the bear for a picnic on a raft in the middle of the lake. But they are interrupted by many croaking frogs who want to join them. The frogs won't stop croaking, so the pig, squirrel, hedgehog, hen, and bear pole away to a quieter spot instead. When they get stuck on a sandbar, they must ask the frogs for help. The frogs come, jumping and croaking, to the rescue. The water picnickers discover that the frogs are good company, in spite of their loud croaking.

The Berenstain Bears Get the Gimmies

by Stan and Jan Berenstain
New York: Random House, 1988

The Berenstain bear cubs get that old gimmie gleam in their eyes every time they get in the checkout line at the supermarket. They whine and scream for everything they see and Mama and Papa bear usually give in to quiet them down. Papa finally explains to the cubs that their behavior is outrageous, disgraceful, and embarrassing. With the help of Gramps and Gran, the family works out a plan to cure the cubs of the galloping greedy gimmies.

Feelings

by Aliki
New York: Greenwillow Books, 1984

A good book about feelings—fabulous pictures and words about feeling sad, happy, jealous, embarrassed, frightened, excited—and many, many more. The drawings are in sections and give an ideal picture of the changing emotions, moods, and feelings of children. Recommended for independent reading.

I Sure Am Glad to See You, Blackboard Bear
by Martha Alexander
New York: Dial Press, 1976

What can Anthony do when his ice cream gets stolen by a bully, Gloria won't share with him, and Joe and Julia tease him? He gets his Blackboard Bear to give him a little help. When Anthony gets ice-cream cones for him and his bear, Stewart, the bully, tries to take one. Well, no one takes Blackboard Bear's blueberry ice-cream cone—his favorite flavor. Anthony sure is glad to see Blackboard Bear when he has to deal with children who are teasing, selfish, or bullying.

It's Mine!
by Leo Lionni
New York: Alfred A. Knopf, 1985

On an island in the middle of Rainbow Pond lived three quarrelsome frogs. Milton insisted that the water belonged to him. Rupert declared that the earth was his. Lydia screamed, "The air is mine!" One day a huge storm darkens the sky and it begins to rain very hard. The island grows smaller and smaller as the water rises. The frightened frogs huddle together on one rock. They joyfully agree that the island belongs equally to them all. This story is a good lesson in sharing.

Just Not the Same
by Addie Lacoe
Boston: Houghton Mifflin, 1992

Three triplets — Cleo, Mirabelle, and Gertrude — couldn't seem to share anything. They couldn't share the front seat in the car, the first apple on the tree, their new triple bunk bed they got for their birthday, or even a new puppy. But their mother teaches the triplets not only how to share, but that sharing can be fun! Cleo, Mirabelle, and Gertrude finally discover how to compromise and share in this well-illustrated storybook about sibling rivalry and sharing.

Mufaro's Beautiful Daughters
by John Steptoe
New York: Lothrop, Lee & Shepard, 1987

Mufaro lived in a village with his two beautiful daughters, Manyara and Nyasha. Manyara was often bad-tempered, while Nyasha was kind to all she met. The King sends word to all the villages that he is in search of the worthiest and most beautiful woman in the land to be his Queen. Mufaro and his daughters must travel to the city to see the King. Manyara rushes ahead of her family in order to be the first to see the King. Nyasha shares her food and kind words with everyone she meets along the journey. Manyara and Nyasha are both surprised by what they find in the city.

A Playhouse for Monster
by Virginia Mueller
Niles, IL: Albert Whitman, 1985

Monster makes a sign for his playhouse that says "KEEP OUT!" "This is MY playhouse," he says. He tells his friend that it's "my window," "my table,"—everything is Monster's. Sitting in his playhouse alone with one cookie and one glass of milk, Monster realizes it is more fun to share than to keep everything for himself. So Monster gets two chairs, two cookies, and two glasses of milk—and a new sign that says "WELCOME!"

Slither McCreep and His Brother, Joe
by Tony Johnston
San Diego: Harcourt Brace Jovanovich, 1992

Slither McCreep's brother Joe won't share anything! He won't share his beach ball or his rat robots or his purple sweater. He even put a sign on his door saying "No Slithers aloud." Even though Joe spelled wrong, Slither was still mad. While Joe sits and watches his favorite band, "Bal Boa and the Vindow Vipers" with his purple sweater wound around his head, Slither McCreep slithers into his brother's room and squeezes everything in sight. Later, he feels bad about squeezing everything and his brother, Joe, feels bad about not sharing anything. They decide to make up and buy something new together.

Want to Play?
by Marissa Moss
Boston: Houghton Mifflin, 1990

Frieda wants to play with her brother, Jonas. But he won't play and won't share his "stuff." Frieda tries and tries to get her brother to play with her, but Jonas is just not interested. When Frieda finds a feather and has a wonderful time playing with it by herself, Jonas wants to trade one of his things for the feather, but Frieda says "no"—she's happy playing. A book about sharing, as well as independence and playing.

What Feels Best?
by Anita Harper
New York: Putnam, 1988

When a young kangaroo gets candy from her grandmother, she eats it all—which doesn't make her feel very good. When she gets a new bike, she doesn't let anyone else ride it—which doesn't make her feel good either. The little kangaroo doesn't share anything, even her feelings, so she just doesn't feel very good at all. So when her mom makes her a cake, she decides to share it, and when she gets a special job from her teacher, she asks her friends to help. She feels a lot better sharing. A good book about sharing things and feelings, as well as helping others.

Index